Using Gemstones to Connect with Your Superpowers!

For Kids and Adults

by Alex Hadassah Anzalone
Illustrations by Nadica Zlatkova M.

Notice: The instructions in this book are not intended to replace recommendations or advice from physicians or other healthcare providers. All internet addresses included in this book were active and appropriate at the time of publication. The author and publisher have no control over and assume no liability for the material on those websites or links on those sites.

To get free bonuses, resources, and other information, visit www.alexanzalone.com

Interior design: Amie Olson

Cover design: Laura Duffy

Illustrations: Nadica Zlatkova M.

Cover and Illustration concepts: Alex Hadassah Anzalone

Model Credits: Amethyst—Noah A., Aquamarine—Nick A., Lapis Lazuli—Chris A., Rose Quartz—Katia A., Tiger's Eye—Nadia A., Citrine—Isabella A., Red Jasper—Jonah A., Chrysocolla— Max A., Others—Noemi and Matisse W., Gianna and Marc A.

ISBN 978-0-692-92593-5 (paperback)
ISBN 978-0-692-97448-3 (e-book)

Dedication

This book is dedicated to all the precious gems in my life:

To my nephews and nieces with whom I have shared my love of crystals and rocks. Thank you for being the inspiration for this book. I love you infinitely.

To my life partner and love of my life, Joshua. Thank you for your incredible love and support. Every day with you is the greatest blessing. You are my hero!

To my three brothers, sisters-in-law, and parents. Thank you for being amazingly loving and supportive, and for giving life to all the little Anzalones! I am beyond grateful to have such a beautiful family.

To Sally. Thank you for being my guide and helping me birth this book! I am forever grateful for your support and belief in me.

To my dear friends. Thank you for your loving and nurturing presence. You inspire me to keep moving forward through life's challenges.

To Grandpa Will Shulman, who was a mineralogist during his life. While he wasn't our biological grandfather, he was a sweet grandfather figure that I admired. He shared his love of stones with my brother and me when we were kids, and that is where my love of rocks and gemstones began. I couldn't help but think of him as I wrote this book.

Nothing can dim the light
which shines from within.

- Maya Angelou

What's Inside

A Note for Parents & Caregivers 7

Introduction 9

Caring for Your Gemstones 11

Clearing Your Gemstones 13

Purple Flame Meditation 15

Moon Cleansing 15

Using Your Gemstones 17

1. Amethyst: peaceful + relaxed 19

2. Aquamarine: calm + cool 21

3. Lapis Lazuli: speak + write with confidence 23

4. Rose Quartz: happy + loving 25

5. Tiger's Eye: courageous + confident 27

6. Citrine: optimistic + creative 29

7. Red Jasper: determination + perseverance 31

8. Chrysocolla: inner strength + resilience 33

A Few Final Notes 35

Other Ways to Use Your Gemstones 37

Journaling Activity 38

My Favorite Gemstone Shops 40

About the Author 41

Parents & Caregivers

Gemstones are a great way to empower children, but are not a replacement for medical advice. Do not leave a young child unattended with gemstones as they can look like candy and present a choking hazard.

With Love,

Alex

Introduction

Gemstones, also known as crystals, are awesome gifts from the Earth! Each crystal has a special energy that helps us remember our superpowers. As a matter of fact, everything on the planet is made up of energy.

We are energy.

Trees and nature are energy.

Animals and insects are energy.

The earth, trees, birds, and bees each have their own energies.

All of nature was designed with a special energy that helps us feel recharged and great. That's why when we walk or play outside or play with our pets, we feel happier, stronger, and more relaxed... It's the healing energy of nature.

Sometimes being human, we forget we are part of nature, and that we have a special glowing energy inside of us, too. Just like a crystal has different sides, or facets, your energy gives you different kinds of superpowers. Some of your superpowers include focus, determination, and courage. Remembering our superpowers makes us feel happier and stronger.

In this book, you will find cool gemstones that you can use to bring out these superpowers and many more. These are just a few of my favorites to get you started, but there are many more for you to explore! Check out "My Favorite Gemstone Shops" on p. 40 to find out where you can buy the gemstones you've seen in this book and many others.

Caring for Your Gemstones

Clearing Your Gemstones

Before you use a gemstone, you need to clear it of energy from others who have held it. Do this whenever you get a new gemstone. After that, do it whenever you think the gemstone needs it. One way to tell if your gemstone needs to be cleared is to hold it in your hand, close your eyes, and take a moment to feel it. As you are doing that, ask yourself whether it needs to be cleared and go with your first guess that comes to mind.

To clear your gemstone, use either the *Purple Flame Meditation* (not a real purple flame—just an imaginary one) or *Moon Cleansing*. Flip to the next page to see how.

Purple Flame Meditation

Find a comfortable place to sit and relax.

Take a moment to connect with your gemstone. Notice how it feels in your hand. Notice its color and shape.

Next, make a little cup with your hands to hold your gemstone. You can close your eyes or keep them open if you prefer.

Imagine a bright purple flame coming out of your hands, surrounding and flowing inside the gemstone. Now imagine the purple flame turning into water, washing away all the old energy from the gemstone, and leaving it clear and clean.

Moon Cleansing

Crystals also enjoy being left on the windowsill with the moon shining on them, especially a full moon. Leave them there overnight and they will be ready to use the next morning.

That's it! You're ready to use your gemstones!

Using Your Gemstones

Amethyst

I am peaceful and relaxed.

I am one with everyone and everything in the Universe.

Superpowers: peaceful + relaxed

Use amethyst when you are feeling anxious or sad. It will activate superpowers that help you feel *peaceful + relaxed.*

How can I use amethyst to activate my superpowers?

With your eyes closed (or open if you prefer), take a deep breath in and out, and imagine this stone helping you feel *peaceful, relaxed, and one with the Universe.*

Bonus: Sleep with amethyst under your pillow for good dreams.

Aquamarine

I am calm and can handle anything that comes my way today.

I got this!

Superpowers: calm + cool

Use aquamarine when you are feeling angry or overwhelmed. It will activate superpowers that help you feel *calm + cool.*

How can I use aquamarine to activate my superpowers?

With your eyes closed (or open if you prefer), take a deep breath in and out, and imagine this stone helping you feel *calm and flow through your day with ease.*

Lapis Lazuli

It is easy for me to speak in front of other people.

I easily express myself in writing.

Superpowers: speak + write with confidence

Use lapis lazuli when you are feeling afraid to speak to others—including family, friends, classmates, or parents. You can also use it if you feel stuck when you are writing. It will activate superpowers that help you *speak + write with confidence.*

How can I use lapis lazuli to activate my superpowers?

With your eyes closed (or open if you prefer), take a deep breath in and out, and imagine this stone helping you feel *confident when you speak and write.*

Rose Quartz

I feel happy and I love myself no matter what.

I get along easily with my friends and other kids at school.

Superpowers: happy + loving

Use rose quartz when you feel sad or upset with yourself or someone else. It will activate superpowers that help you feel *happy + loving.*

How can I use rose quartz to activate my superpowers?

With your eyes closed (or open if you prefer), take a deep breath in and out, and imagine this stone helping you feel *happy, loving, and connected to others.*

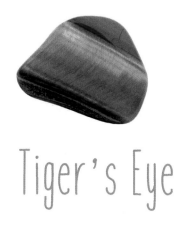

Tiger's Eye

I am courageous like a tiger!

I am confident and succeed at whatever I put my mind to.

Superpowers: courageous + confident

Use tiger's eye when you feel scared or shy. It will activate superpowers that help you feel *courageous + confident.*

How can I use tiger's eye to activate my superpowers?

With your eyes closed (or open if you prefer), take a deep breath in and out, and imagine this stone is helping you feel *courageous and confident.*

Citrine

I am optimistic!

I always find ways to have fun and enjoy life!

Superpowers: optimistic + creative

Use citrine when you feel negative or bored. It will activate superpowers that help you feel *optimistic + creative.*

How can I use citrine to activate my superpowers?

With your eyes closed (or open if you prefer), take a deep breath in and out, and imagine this stone is helping you feel *optimistic and creative.*

Red Jasper

I am determined to get my work done!

I am willing to work hard to accomplish my goals.

Superpowers: determination + perseverance

Use red jasper when you lack motivation and willpower. It will activate super-powers for *determination + perseverance* to help you accomplish whatever you set your mind to.

How can I use red jasper to activate my superpowers?

With your eyes closed (or open if you prefer), take a deep breath in and out, and imagine this stone is helping you feel *determined to persevere so that you can accomplish your goals.*

Chrysocolla

I ride the waves of life with ease.

My feelings are like the waves of an ocean...

They come and go and I let them flow.

Superpowers: inner strength + resilience

Use chrysocolla when you want to let difficult emotions flow away. It will activate superpowers for *inner strength + resilience* to help you overcome changes or challenges.

How can I use chrysocolla to activate my superpowers?

With your eyes closed (or open if you prefer), take a deep breath in and out, and imagine this stone is helping you feel *inner strength to deal with changes and challenges. Now imagine your challenging feelings flowing away.*

Bonus: You can also imagine yourself riding a wave like a pro and having a fun time while doing it!

A Few Final Notes

Other Ways to Use Your Gemstones

**Here are some other ways that you can use your gemstones
to remind you of your superpowers:**

- Carry your favorite gemstone in your pocket, backpack, or purse.

- Put your favorite gemstone under your pillow when you sleep at night.

- Keep your gemstone next to your bed.

- Keep your gemstone on your desk while you work, write, or create art.

- Lie down and put your gemstone on your heart, above your belly button, or in the middle of your forehead.

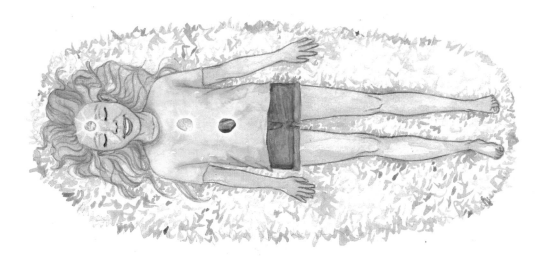

Journaling Activity

I hope you've enjoyed your journey through this book! There are so many more amazing gemstones for you to explore. Remember, you have special super-powers inside of you that you can use to make your life shine brighter. Anytime you start to forget, use your gemstones to remind you!

What are your 3 favorite gemstones in this book?

1. _____

2. _____

3. _____

What are your 3 favorite superpowers?

1. _____

2. _____

3. _____

How did using the gemstone meditations help you?

_____

_____

_____

What superpowers did you begin to develop in yourself?

_____

_____

_____

How will you use gemstones in the future to develop your superpowers?

_____

_____

_____

Have fun with your gemstones!

Love,
XO

Alex

My Favorite Gemstone Shops

Buy In Person

Crystal Essence, Great Barrington, MA
www.crystalessence.com

Buy Online or In Person

Tushita Heaven, Saratoga Springs, NY
www.tushitaheaven.com

Note: If you prefer to visit a store that is closer to where you live, search Google for a crystal shop in your area. When shopping for gemstones, ask for "tumbled stones." They are the most affordable and easiest to carry around. If you can't find a gemstone that you see in this book, feel free to substitute with one of a similar color.

Gemstone Resources

The Encyclopedia of Crystals by Judy Hall

The Crystal Healer by Philip Permutt

About Alex

Alex Hadassah Anzalone is a gemstone lover, Integrative Nutrition Health Coach, Kundalini Yoga Instructor, and former New York Attorney. After many years of using gemstones for healing and empowerment and sharing them with friends and family, Alex designed this book to share both the stunning beauty and gentle healing quality of gemstones with kids and adults.

For free bonuses, more information, and additional resources on where to buy gemstones, visit www.alexanzalone.com

Made in the USA
Middletown, DE
07 July 2020